THE CAROLERS
GEORGIA GUBACK

Greenwillow Books New York

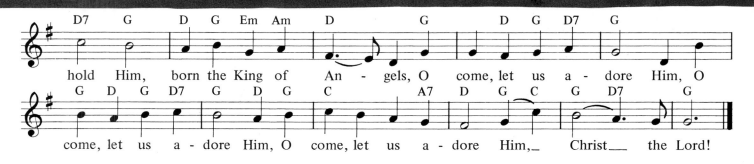

hold Him, born the King of An - gels, O come, let us a - dore Him, O

come, let us a - dore Him, O come, let us a - dore Him,__ Christ__ the Lord!

To my guardian angel

The full-color art was done as cut-paper collage.   Copyright © 1992 by Georgia Guback. All rights reserved.
No part of this book may be reproduced or utilized in any form or by any means, electronic or mechanical, including
photocopying, recording, or by any information storage and retrieval system, without permission in writing from
the Publisher, Greenwillow Books, a division of William Morrow & Company, Inc., 1350 Avenue of the Americas,
New York, NY 10019. Printed in Singapore by Tien Wah Press.   First Edition   10 9 8 7 6 5 4 3 2 1

Library of Congress Cataloging-in-Publication Data
Guback, Georgia.   The carolers/by Georgia Guback.   p.   cm.
   Summary: Follows a group of carolers from house to house as they share with others the beauty of Christmas.
Includes lyrics and music from the carols they are singing.   ISBN 0-688-09772-3 (trade).   ISBN 0-688-09773-1 (lib.)
[1. Christmas — Fiction.   2. Stories without words.]   I. Title.   PZ7.G9343Car   1992   [E] — dc20
90-41756   CIP   AC

bove thy deep and dream-less sleep the si-lent stars go by; Yet

in thy dark streets shin - eth the ev - er - last - ing Light; The

hopes and fears of all the years are met in thee to - night.

The — first — No - el, the— an - gel did say, Was to cer - tain poor

sheep, On a cold win - ter's night __ that was __ so deep. No - el, ___ No -

el, No - el, No - el, Born is the King of Is - ra - el.

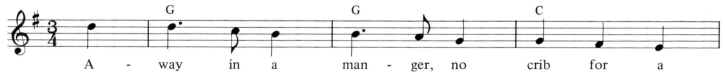

A - way in a man - ger, no crib for a

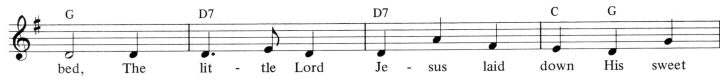

bed, The lit - tle Lord Je - sus laid down His sweet

head.   The   stars   in   the   sky_____   looked   down   where   He

lay, The lit - tle Lord Je - sus, a - sleep on the hay.

mer - cy mild,___ God and sin - ners rec - on - ciled!" Joy - ful, all ye na - tions rise,___

join the tri-umph of the skies;_ With th'an-gel-ic host pro-claim, "Christ is_ born in

Beth - le - hem!" Hark! the her - ald an - gels sing, "Glo - ry__ to the new - born King!"

WE THREE

We three kings of O-ri-ent are; Bear-ing gifts we tra-verse a-

...KINGS OF ORIENT ARE; BEARING...

far, Field and foun-tain, moor and moun-tain, Fol-low-ing yon-der Star.

O__ Star of won - der, Star of night, Star with roy - al beau - ty bright,

West - ward lead - ing, still pro - ceed - ing, Guide us to Thy per - fect Light.

Si - lent night! ho - ly night! All is calm,

all   is   bright 'Round yon Vir - gin Moth - er and   Child,

Ho - ly In - fant so ten - der and mild, Sleep in heav - en - ly

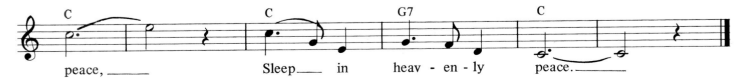

peace, _____ Sleep__ in heav - en - ly peace. _____

IT CAME UPON A MIDNIGHT

It came up-on a mid-night clear, that glo-ri-ous song of old, From

an - gels bend - ing near the earth to touch their harps of gold; "Peace

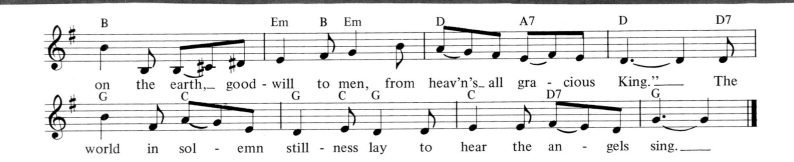

WHAT CHILD IS THIS, WHO,

What Child is this,_ Who, laid to rest,_ on Mar - y's lap_ is sleep - ing? Whom

an - gels greet_ with an - thems sweet,_while shep - herds watch_ are keep - ing?

LAID TO REST, ON MARY'S LAP . . .

This, this is Christ the King, Whom shep-herds guard and an - gels sing;

Haste, haste to bring Him laud, the Babe, the Son of Mar - y.

room,_____ And heav'n and na - ture_____ sing, and__ heav'n and na - ture_____
sing, And __ heav'n __ and heav'n _____ and na - ture sing.